CASCADING HEARTS

CASCADING HEARTS

WRITTEN BY
JUSTINE DAVID

ILLUSTRATIONS BY
JOLI NOELLE DAVID

CASCADING HEARTS

ISBN: 978-0-692-89620-4

Some characters and events in this book are fictitious. Any resemblance to real
persons, living or dead, is coincidental and not intended by the author.

Cover image and illustrations by Joli Noelle David
Interior design by Justine David

justinepdavid@gmail.com
instagram.com/justinepdavid

For all who have touched my heart,

I am a culmination of pieces of you.

I. THE FALL

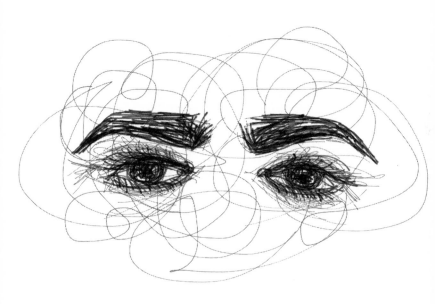

HOCUS POCUS

Your mind is full of so much magic.
    I find myself lost in it when you speak.

The way you think is like
    nothing I've ever known,
    or heard,
    or ever before seen.

I love watching you try to explain
    all the happenings in your head.

Although they can be difficult to follow,
    your thoughts have me under your spell.

TURNING POINT

From the moment I saw those bright, curious eyes, I knew my life would never be the same...and for once, I didn't want it to be.

SWEET SYMPHONY

There is no more captivating sound
than that of a lover's laugh.

Even sweeter is the thought
that my humor had that impact.

SECRET MEMORIES

I remember one time you texted me drunk.
You said *I love you, marry me, die with me.*

I knew your words held no meaning.
I dismissed them, but my heart still fell.
So I quietly tucked that memory away.

At one point in time, no matter how fleeting,
the thought of you and me forever crossed your mind,
and that alone never fails to make me smile.

IN DREAMS YOU WILL LOSE YOUR HEARTACHES

A dream is a wish your heart makes.
Last night I dreamt of you.

PHOTOGRAPH

Trying to capture
    all of your beauty
    in a single photograph
    is like taking a picture
    of the full moon at night—
    gorgeous, but never quite
    as stunning as it is
    without the barrier
    of a camera lens.

SECRET AFFAIR

There were times I had to look away from you,
  like when you'd lick your lips,
  or roll your hips.

I had to avoid the impending scene
  of me taking you on your dining table
  in front of all your friends;

Spreading your legs with me in between,
  kissing every inch of you
  and making you scream.

You told me, *the trick is to not look too long or too hard,*
  but all I could think about was
  fucking you for too long and incredibly hard.

BODIES

His hands wandered through
the curves of my body ever so slowly.

His eyes took me in with such awe,
and in that moment,
my insecurities disappeared
and it was just me and him—
two naked bodies,
carrying two very different souls.

It would never work out between us,
but how lovely it is to just lay in bed
and admire the human body.

TREMBLE

Her touch can soothe the sorest pain
    and make the strongest legs tremble.

FALLING ALL OVER AGAIN

I'm being dragged back down to hell
    and I'm holding the devil's hand as I go.

I can't help myself
    because the empty promises
    whispered in my ear
    sound so much sweeter
    the second time around.

SLOWLY

I love making you mine—
    kissing the back of your neck,
    lips tracing down your spine,
    gently biting on your hip,
    taking my sweet, sweet time.

SKIPPING BEATS

Do you know that feeling of falling—when you're dropping down on a roller coaster or when there's really bad turbulence on a plane or even when you're falling off of a building in your dreams? I get that same sensation in my heart every time our eyes meet. It feels like I'm literally falling for you.

SILK

Your voice sounds how silk feels,
    smooth and sexy.

WOMAN DOWN

I fell in love with you a long time ago,
      and I don't think I ever got back up.

LMJ

Black hair, green eyes, red lips,
    thick brows, nose ring, curvy hips.

Leather jacket, lace choker, silk dress,
    heads turn, hearts fall, such finesse.

Fervent voice, brilliant mind, noble goals,
    brave spirit, loving heart, passionate soul.

Sweet disposition,
    pained with apprehension.

Some will love, some will hate,
    either way, hearts will break.

GAME ON

I felt your stares from across the room
      as I pretended to be indifferent,

But believe me when I say,
      every move I made was deliberate.

ORGANIC CHEMISTRY

I want to meet someone I have organic chemistry with. The raw connection you instantly spark with a stranger you meet for the very first time.

Unedited, no pressure, nothing to lose.

HOPELESS

Many have tried,
    all fell to defeat.

To not love her,
    an impossible feat.

JELLO

How do you do that?
That thing with your eyes
that makes my legs feel weak.

RUSH

You drive me crazy
    with your eager sex eyes,
    dark and dripping with lust.

All becomes hazy,
    your face between my thighs,
    my hips aching to thrust.

WINDOWS

You have the most captivating eyes I have ever seen.
They look at the world with so much curiosity,
as if every aspect of living fascinates you.

I want to know every single thought that crosses your mind.
I have a feeling it will be very enlightening,
and will also cause me to fall even harder than I already have.

Tell me what you're thinking, I'm ready.

FOREPLAY

Lingering stares from across the table;
    calculated, discreet grazes of skin.

A whiff of her perfume,
    heat building up within.

She bites her lip,
    I lick mine.

Tension building up in the air.

There's something so damn thrilling
    about this secret affair.

BUTTERFLIES

You make me nervous,
    I'm not sure why.

Maybe it's because deep down
    my heart knows
    you're going to break it.

II. THE PAIN

DOUBTS

Sometimes I wonder if any of it was real,
    if you felt even an ounce of the love you claimed.

Could it be that I just imagined the ideal,
    while you spoke lies and loved another unashamed?

OUT OF MY MIND

You say that I'm crazy,
    but baby I'm just crazy for you.

LOVE STORY

I've felt a deep, consuming, impassioned love once in my life.

It was the kind of love that emanated from the deep trenches of my soul. I felt it in every cell of my body, from the neurons in my brain to the myocytes in my little pinky toe.

It was the kind of love that I wasn't even aware existed. I felt it flood into my life all at once, as if it were God granting the prayers of those in a drought.

It was the kind of love that killed me, only to revive me the next second. I felt my eyes burn with jealousy, and harsh words pierce my skin through to my heart. Then I felt the softest lips in the world caress my wounds.

It was the kind of passion that was depicted in the most romantic of movies; dramatic proclamations of love and empty promises were exchanged—

I will never stop loving you, I will never leave you.

But unlike the movies, this love did not have a happy ending. This love faded as the sun does set.

I felt it dissipate in every missed call,
in every message left on *Read*,
in every cancelled date,
in every hollow I miss you too.

I felt the rejection so strongly that the love eventually became a distant memory. And just like that, the love that ignited my heart, was gone.

I've felt a deep, consuming, impassioned heartbreak once in my life.

NO HEARTSTRINGS ATTACHED

You asked me,
> *Why can't you just let me love you?*

I sighed in frustration because I knew
    that more than just simply love
    you had no intention to do.

BETWEEN THE NOTES

There are memories buried in the melodies of songs she used to play.
I now have a playlist entitled *DO NOT PLAY.*

INTERSECTION

Her face, illuminated with a reddish hue;
    tension consuming all the air.

Regret overcomes me as soon as my words pour out,
    I still love you the same, nothing for me has changed.

Her eyes, lost in the dewy drops of the windshield of her car;
    from her silence I knew,

That for her it was different,
    this love she outgrew.

The glow on her skin turns green,
    and with that, we move forward,
    my heart torn in two.

UNREQUITED

I know I can't have you,
    but the love that I feel for you
    has amassed in my heart.

With nowhere to go,
    it eventually became
    the lump in my throat.

VIRTUAL LOVE

1/7/15
8:32 am Babe <3 : Good morning beautiful, I hope you have a
wonderful day. I'll be thinking of you, I love you!!
9:05 am Me: Good morning!! Have fun at work, I miss you and I
love you soooooo much :D
9:07 am Babe <3: Call me when you can, I miss you too :) Drive
safe <3

2/23/15
1:18 pm Babe <3: Hey gorgeous, I miss you so much. I can't stop
thinking about you. Call me when you get out of class <3
1:19 pm Me: You're so cute :)) 3 more months until I can have you
in my arms again. I love you baby, I'll call you in a bit

3/11/15
3:02 am Babe <3: I miss your lips...
3:05 am Me: I want you so bad right now
3:05 am Babe <3: Fuck, I wish I could be there with you baby
3:06 am Me: Trust me, I wish you were here right now too. The
things I'd do to you...
3:06 am Babe <3: Fuck. Me.

4/4/15
2:23pm Me: I saw THE cutest little Husky at work this morning
and I thought of you. Don't worry, you're much much cuter ;) love
youu!
2:30 pm Babe <3: Lol you're fuckin cute. I love you baby, thinking
of you aaaall day

5/23/15
9:41 pm Me: How was work? I miss you!!
11:17 pm Babe <3: Good. I'm really tired, let's talk tomorrow

5/28/15
12:47 pm Babe <3: Sorry can't talk. At work
12:53 pm Me: Okay, I'll call you later?

6/7/15
5:12 pm Me: Hi can I call you? I miss your voice...
8:46 pm Babe <3: I've been really busy lately. Talk to you soon

6/15/15
7:57 am Me: OMG three more days...I can't wait to see you! I love and miss you so fucking much.
10:10 am Babe <3: Miss u too

10/4/15
11:49 pm Me: I found some of your clothes in my closet. I guess I'll just mail it to you?
10/5/15
8:07 am DNC: Yea that's fine
9:22 am Me: ok

12/31/15
11:56 pm Me: yuor thee olny thng I can thnikk abot rite now
11:56 pm Me: I misss u I stil lovee yuo
Read

FORGOTTEN

Remember when you said that you will always love me?
    I do.

A LIFETIME AGO

Your soft, tender lips instantly invade my thoughts when people ask,
Have you ever been in love?

IRREVERSIBLE

There's nothing more heartbreaking than witnessing the passion fade from your lover's eyes, when there's absolutely nothing you can do to stop it.

PINKY PROMISE

I promised you that you'd always be in my life. The last time I saw you was one year, two months, and five days ago.

I still hear your voice in the songs you used to sing.
I still see your smirk when someone makes a sexual innuendo.
I still feel your body in tight hugs that last a little too long.
I still smell your shampoo in strangers' hair flowing in the wind.
I still taste you in my favorite drink.

I just don't tell you anymore.

LEFT UNSAID

I think you underestimated just how much I loved you,
    but I guess I have some fault in that.

I never told you how your laugh was the most mesmerizing
    sound I had ever heard,
    or how your paradoxical mind constantly fascinated me,
    or how the thought of your existence calmed my soul.

I never told you how fast my heart would beat whenever I'd
    see your name on my phone,
    or how much my face would ache after our six-hour phone
    calls, or how much you turned me on with just a few words.

I never told you that I began to see beauty all around me after I met
    you, or that I became the best version of me I've ever been,
    or that I saw the rest of my life with you by my side.

I never told you because I knew you didn't love me the same way.

INTOLERABLE

Do you know what it feels like to lose something you never had?
It feels impossible.

TRANSITION STATE

Our loneliness matched. Maybe that's why we fell so hard for each other. That was only temporary because I was just a placeholder for someone better for you.

MISSING

I miss the you that I fell so madly in love with,
      but that person doesn't exist anymore—
      maybe never even did.

WALLS

She once met a boy who told her,
you make me curious, I want to get to know your head.

When she finally allowed herself to be read,
the boy lost all interest and fled.

She then vowed to always keep her walls up high
and never let anyone in ever again.

OXYMORON

I never understood the fine line between love and hate...
    until I met you.

BITTERSWEET

You once said you felt proud
    to have caused the wetness between my thighs.

Tell me, how did you feel
    to have often done the same to my eyes.

SIXTH SENSE

You were never just another face. The first time I saw you was unlike anything I've ever felt. It was an incomparable feeling. I had this strange awareness of who we were going to be to each other. It was as if you broke my heart before you even said hello.

ONE CHANCE

I think the scariest part of letting someone go is the thought that this exciting feeling of love is limited and will never happen again, as if love and all its parts have been tainted with the essence of them, and that no one, in the population of seven billion humans on this planet, can recreate the passion and tenderness that the two of you shared, because what you had with that person was special—so special that all the kisses and butterflies inside of you were solely reserved for them.

These are the ramblings in my head that terrify me into holding on.

NOTHING NEW

This song reminds me of you,
    you once told me,
    and her,
    and her,
    and her.

MISS ME

Does she kiss you the way I do—
    tenderly in the morning
    and hungrily at night?

Does she make you feel good like I used to—
    crazy good sex,
    while holding you tight?

Tell me, does she treat you right—
    love you like no other,
    with no one else in sight?

MURPHY'S LAW

Anything that can go wrong, will go wrong.

I like to believe that this adage was penned from witnessing a love like ours.

LEFTOVERS

I write to spill the remnants of you out of my system.

III. THE REMEDY

CAFÉ

A coffee shop
    filled with sleepless students,
    new lovers,
    and lost writers.

Somehow I feel less alone
    in a room full of strangers.
    Their presence is oddly calming,
    drawing out the heartache in me.

FOOLISH

I wholeheartedly believed the words I said
    when we were naked, snuggled up in your bed.

I can't live without you, I whispered,
    but the look in your eyes
    I gravely misconstrued.

What I thought to be tenderness, was just guilt unheard,
    because you knew you couldn't reciprocate
    the love I'd always exude.

Now here I am, living without you,
    doing the things I thought I couldn't do.

I will forever be grateful for us back then.
    Thanks to you,
    I'll never believe those silly little words ever again.

ALL'S FAIR IN LOVE AND FANTASY

I thought I was in love with you.
    Little did I know then,
    I was in love with the you
    I created in my head.

THE FLOOD

I was drowning in incessant thoughts of you—
    what you were doing,
    who you were with,
    who was making you laugh,
    how you were feeling,
    if you were happy, sad, or mad,
    if you drank enough water, and
    if you were taking all your meds.
    You.
    You.
    You.
    Non-stop.

As time passed, and you finally faded from my thoughts,
    my heart felt so much lighter
    and my mind so much clearer.

BAD DAY

There are days when I miss you,
    but they don't cripple me like they used to.

When I see something that reminds me of you,
    I think about sending you a message,
    just as a friend.

Trust me when I say,
    it takes quite a bit of effort
    not to hit send.

FORGIVEN

I will never forget
    how your words
    made me feel loved
    and lifted my mood.

I will never forget
    how they broke my heart,
    and shattered me too.

CLEAR

Sometimes I wish it would've worked out between us, but then I instantly remember how horribly you treated me, and I think to myself, *oh thank god that never went anywhere.*

ALMOST YOU

For so long I believed
     that it was you to which my heart
     was destined to belong,

Only to discover
     that it was just the potential of you
     that wrongly made me fall.

HOW IT WAS SUPPOSED TO BE

I lost myself to the romanticization of the love story we were in. I was so focused on maintaining the perfect narrative, that I failed to stay true to myself and was consequently blinded to our incompatibility. We fought through many obstacles, but reality inevitably set in and revealed the disparity in our hopeless relationship. We were never meant to spend the rest of our lives together the way we so confidently planned. We were only supposed to cross paths and say:

Oh hello, what a lovely soul you are, but alas, I am not for you as you are not for me. So continue on with your life without me, and I hope you find where you're truly supposed to be.

ETERNAL BEAUTY

You will always be beautiful to me,
    as I have seen your soul.

And although we don't talk anymore,
    I just needed you to know:

Your beauty continues to haunt me,
    and all the others to whom you showed.

BACTERIA

No matter how hard I tried, alcohol could not fill the emptiness you left in me. The only thing that freed me from absolute misery was feeling every aching pain to its highest degree until I gradually developed a resistance to it—like bacteria, developing a natural resistance to antibiotics if you don't finish your prescription. After I felt all that I could feel from my aching heart, I was free to start a new life. Now, I am immune to the likes of you.

AGE SOMETIMES MATTERS

One sign of incompatibility is when one person is exactly where they want to be in life and the other is not even close.

THE OTHER SIDE

She found beauty in the aftermath of a love mourned—
    after shots of vodka and liters of wine have been poured,
    after drunken calls have been made and scorned,

After tears drenched pillows, couches, and comforting shoulders,
    after numerous breakdowns and loss of all composure,

After her newfound distrust of all romance,
    after denials of desperate pleas for *one more chance.*

After all that had passed,
    there it lay,
    the greener grass.

MISTAKEN

The only thing we ever had in common was that we both thought we were in love with each other.

TOXIC

I don't hate you. I hate the relationship I had with you.
Never again...

CAUTION

Don't let words mislead you. Their *I love you* may not be of the same magnitude as yours. Count on their character, not on their promises.

PRE-REQUISITE

I feel so silly for having believed
    that you were the one for me.

I'm so glad I finally outgrew
    the love I thought I knew,

But you were an important lesson,
    so that I can find a love
    I will never have to question.

RED FLAG

One major red flag of a toxic person is when they regulate the amount of love they give you. For example, not giving you the affection you crave because they "don't want to spoil you with too much or else you'll keep expecting it"—like you're some kind of dog who will beg for more and more treats. If they truly love you, then they should believe that you deserve all the love in the world and give you as much of it as they can—not love in increments.

ROSE

A rose blooms gracefully,
    then wilts until it's gone.

As does love ever so quietly,
    in cold, distant summers,
    and in the eyes of lost lovers.

Eventually spring will dawn
    and a new flower will spawn.

The moment will surely come,
    when you've truly moved on.

THE BAADER-MEINHOF PHENOMENON

The greatest ruse my mind has played
    was the fantasy of you and me as fate—
    your song for me on the radio,
    and your name in every show,

Our chance encounter at the club,
    and promises of forever love.
    I believed we were meant to be,
    the signs everywhere around me.

For so long I believed this tale,
    blind to the reality under a veil.
    It was Baader-Meinhof at its finest—
    selective attention and confirmation bias.

We were never written in the stars,
    just two people healing their scars.
    I have finally accepted our goodbye,
    but my dear,
    you were such a beautiful lie.

IV. THE JOURNEY

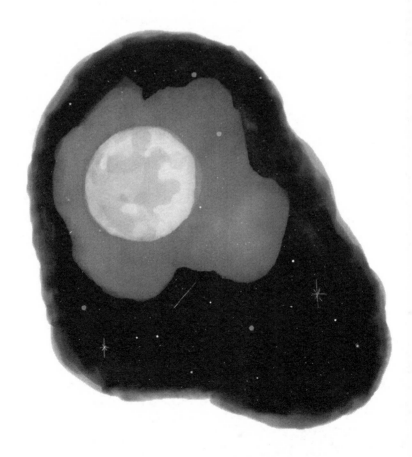

TO NEPTUNE AND BACK

People like to romanticize the moon,
    I've always wondered why.

I guess it's because it can turn the tides,
    and uncover the truth at night,

But I like to daydream about Neptune,
    the furthest planet from this existence.

Life, worlds away, sounds opportune,
    when all in my head is reminiscence—

Of my mistakes, regrets, and aching wounds.
    I long to find peace in all that distance.

AFTERMATH OF A STORM

The incessant drips of rain
    sound like something unfinished.

Reminds me of all my pain,
    something that has yet to be diminished.

MOTIVATION

Am I driven by love,
    or by the hope of its reciprocation?

INSOMNIAC

Lying awake with my eyes closed;
　　　this is what my nights have become.

Forcing my eyes to shut out the world,
　　　only to have my mind come undone.

FRACTIONS

I don't believe that someone out there is my better half. I have to be whole before I can give them all of me.

SHAKESPEAREAN

To be or not to be,
    Hamlet's internal war.

These words echoed within me
    as I dreamed of something more.

I was caught in this same fight;
    take arms against a sea of troubles?

Or drop my weapons and take flight,
    to a place where nothing is,
    and my mind is completely quiet.

Where my soul can be at peace,
    away from this internal riot.

SUNRISE

A new masterpiece painted every hour,
as the sky is the sun's canvas.

For if not blinded, a new day
is more than the sun will grant us.

MUSIC

Music has a way of healing the soul and softening the heart. So pause, take a seat, and let it reverberate through the saddest parts of you.

SOLITUDE'S PREDICAMENT

I am afraid that my loneliness
      has transformed into a magnet.

It'll wrap around me
      and attract the closest thing
      that will make me feel
      anything other than lonely.

CELESTIAL

When you feel like you're drowning in your own thoughts, look up at the stars and let the vastness of space overwhelm you. For a moment, your problems will seem insignificant compared to the grandeur of the night sky. Spend some time staring into space and contemplating your existence and what truly matters to you. Everything will feel lighter in the morning.

CRACKS

I have cracks in my soul
    that are inevitable in life.

I fill them with film and poetry
    to feel more alive inside.

WHAT I FEAR

When I was younger, I had nightmares
 so terrifying I was afraid to go to bed.

Now that I'm twenty-two, the only thing I fear
 are the monsters inside my head.

They tell me life has no meaning,
 and that I'd be better off dead.

So I constantly remind myself
 there are better things ahead.

I've yet to see all the beauty in this world,
 difficult to comprehend.

Despite my demons, I will live and love,
 until my timely inevitable end.

CONDITIONAL

If anyone ever tells you something along the lines of:
Never say never because you might change your mind in the future,
don't ever believe them when they say things like,
I will always love you.

Their *always* means nothing—they might just "change their mind in the future".

ALTERNATE UNIVERSE

I was existing in this world, but I was really living inside my head.

INCOMPARABLE

Compare yourself to who you were yesterday, not to the people living in your phone. The path they're taking is different from yours. Pave your own journey. Revolutionize your world with fearless decisions, motivated by your life's unprecedented adventure.

LET GO

Sometimes you just have to drive with your windows down and let your hand ride the waves of the wind.

NO REASON

Sometimes I don't have an answer to the question,
Why are you sad?

Sometimes I just am. There's not always a reason for my sadness.
It's something I feel intermittently. It's like how some people are
happy for no reason. They just are.

MARKETING AND ADVERTISING

I don't know how to date. The last time I went on a date felt too much like I was trying to sell myself.

What do you do for fun?

I enjoy reading and watching movies. I also know how to cook a mean steak and I've been told that I'm great company at concerts and music festivals. Just pay me with some love and affection.

WAVE OPTICS EXPLAINED BY MY PHYSICS PROFESSOR

Light is a wave. It will bend around a person standing in a spotlight. So even if you're in their shadow, you can still see the light.
    —Dr. Collins

CURIOSITY KILLED THE FANTASY

I wonder what it feels like
    to be loved as hard as I love.

Would I revel in the feeling,
    or run away in fear...

JUST LIKE HER

His smile was deceiving,
  his deep voice alluring.

He said I was funny,
  that he understood me.

You're so amazing, he says,
  You're not like other girls.

How foolish of him to believe
  that it would flatter me to be
  something other than she.

As if there's something wrong
  with being caring, clever, and strong.

I would love to be like other girls,
  who love hard and change peoples' worlds.

Although we can feel insecure at times,
  we don't need to compare penis size.

COMFORTABLE

Are you deep in love,
    with one you see no one else above?
    Or are you afraid to be alone,
    accustomed to a love you've always known?

Not daring to let go and be vulnerable
    to the loneliness that can consume hearts,
    and would rather just remain comfortable—
    safe in your relationship and all its parts.

I hope you're confident in your decision
    to stay where you feel content.
    I hope it's the life you've always envisioned,
    and that you live out your heart's intent.

V. Love

HOME-BOUND

As we lay snuggled on her bed,
    our eyes locked—deep with adoration.

Our legs flowed through the rivers of the silk sheets.
    Her hands explored every curve and turn of my body,
    while my fingertips traced the valley of her cheekbones.

I remember telling myself that this was it for me;
    by her side was where I found my home.

LOST KISSES

I had my first kiss when I was seventeen. I waited until I was in
college to decide that it was okay to have another's lips on mine.

It was a sloppy, drunken kiss with a boy from the room below me.
To say that I was underwhelmed is quite the understatement.
And so I kissed another boy in my inebriated state.
And another,
and another,
and another—
each kiss depreciating in value as they occurred.

I further tried to convince myself that it was the roughness of their
lips and the aggression in their tongues that was so unappealing.
So I decided to kiss a pretty girl at a club, only to be left with that
familiar feeling of discontent.

It was not until I felt the gentle pressure of the softest lips I've ever
known against mine, that I decided that kissing really is as amazing
as they depict it to be in movies and books, if not more.

These lips belonged to someone I fell in love with
after trading countless longing glances,
after trading our most sheltered secrets,
after trading our cascading hearts.

This was when I realized that a kiss is only true, when shared with a
soul connected to your own.

LONG DISTANCE

Thousands of miles away,
    yet I've never felt closer to anyone else.

WILD AT HEART

My mind is me;
>   all the thoughts that I think are mine,
>   but my savage heart is not as tame.

It chose to belong to you,
>   and runs wild at the sound of your name.

WARMTH

Will you let me kiss every freckle on your face,
    and keep you in my warm embrace?

Eyes locked on eyes, with our fingers interlaced.
    I'll kiss your knuckles nice and slow,
    promise to never let you go.

MAKING LOVE TO YOU

When I stare into those deep emerald eyes,
    I get lost in a sea of fantasy.

When you smile, bite your lip, and spread your thighs,
    I fall into a trance of pure ecstasy.

When I hear the sound of your raspy moans,
    I melt into your arms and all is blurred.

When you kiss my lips, I get chills to the bone,
    the world stops, and only beating hearts are heard.

PEACE

I believe that there is no more peaceful moment
in the history of time than the moment when I
wake up wrapped tightly in your arms.

WHERE THE WILD MINDS GO

Sometimes when I see you doing normal things like baking a cake, or applying your make-up, I can't help but stare.

Your beauty is too much to process with just one look. I wonder if you're even real because I cannot fathom such perfection.

I like taking my time admiring
the intensity in your eyes when you focus on whatever it is you're doing,
and the accentuation of your cheekbones,
which must've been sculpted by God himself.

I can't help but marvel at your cute little button nose and the plumpness of your lips.
God, those lips.
I love how I can feel how soft they are just by looking at them.

I can't help but gape at the smoothness of your neck,
as I imagine my mouth gliding over it.

Then suddenly, I'm snapped back into reality,
and I want my hands all over you.

OUR SONG

Sing to me, my love;
    let the music in you
    be the rhythm of my heartbeat.

Let the soul in your song
    be in harmony with my own.

EXPLORATION

I want to feel every inch of you
underneath my fingertips,
and in between my lips.

NEON SOUL (prompt by Alexandra Elle)

My soul recognizes you.
 It glows bright,
 and feels like neon when you're around,
 as if excitedly alerting me of
 the presence of its mate.

EAGER

You deserve the kind of love that you're so eager to give to others.

UTOPIA

My face belongs in the crook of your neck,
 and my arms around your waist,
 as my fingertips trace over your tattoos,
 with our legs interlaced.

You are my paradise.

CRAVE

The degree to which I crave you can never be fully satiated. I'll always want more of you—even when I already have you snuggled in my arms.

HANDS

Your hands are the key to my undoing—
    strip me of my troubles,
    roam my body,
    take me down,
    unravel me.

XXVII

She loves hard.

You can see it in the way
she speaks with her hands waving around,
as if words aren't enough
to express all that's within.

You can feel it in the way
she puts her words together
to inspire young hearts,
and call people to action.

You can hear it in the way
she sings with her eyes closed,
as if trying to contain
all the tears she is repressing.

I hope she's aware of her worth,
and that her existence is such a blessing.

THE BUTTERFLY EFFECT

The day I met you,
I had butterflies in my stomach.

They flapped their wings,
then days later,
I found myself drowning
in a tsunami of love
for you.

TE AMO

Mi amor por ti
trasciende el idioma Inglés,
y sangra en Español.

(*My love for you
transcends the English language,
and bleeds into Spanish.*)

ADORBSY

The cutest thing I've ever seen is when you'd bury your face in my chest in embarrassment every time you'd say something really dirty; that, and puppies.

VOWS

Elated, enraged, blue,
    or insane,

I vow to cherish you
    all the same.

LIGHT BULB

It's fascinating how one light bulb
can create such a drastic change
in a pitch-black room.

It's like the difference between
captivity and freedom;

Trapped in the darkness
of my own mind,
only to be liberated
by one single thought of you—
my source of light.

IF YOU WANT SOMETHING DONE RIGHT, DO IT YOURSELF

People always say that "you have to love yourself before you can love anyone else". For me, the opposite happened. I learned how to love myself after loving someone who wasn't capable of loving me the way I so desired.

JUST ONE

Take yourself out on a date, and experience who you are wholly. Go to the theaters, watch a movie, and laugh uninhibitedly or cry with snot running from your nose, while also trying to regain proper breathing (aka ugly cry). Pick a city you've always dreamed of visiting and book a ticket. Explore a new world by yourself, and you'll learn that you're actually a really fun person to spend time with. Learn to love yourself, then you'll never be alone.

SELF-LOVE

Don't let your life become a series of regrets and missed opportunities. Do what you need to do to become the person you've always wanted to be. You'll love yourself so much for being fearless and doing what makes you happy. Ignite your soul with your fiery passion and let that light guide you to your paradise.

AUTHOR'S NOTE

Dearest reader,

There are probably a hundred different reasons why you in particular have this book in your hands. Maybe a friend gifted it to you because you're still not over your ex, and this is their way of telling you to get your shit together. Or maybe you're like me, and you're in love with the idea of love. Or maybe you just thought the cover looks nice. Whatever the reason may be, I hope these pages were able to elicit any deep feelings you may be harboring, as they have truly done for me. I also hope that this was an enjoyable experience for you, because what you are currently holding is a piece of my soul—a horcrux, if you will. So, thank you for the time you have spent with a piece of me. It truly means the world.

Love, with all my pieces,
    Jus

INDEX

Made in the USA
San Bernardino, CA
10 September 2017